His Majesty the King

Written by Ruth Corrin
Illustrated by Marc Mongeau

CelebrationPress
An Imprint of ScottForesman

"It's a beautiful night," said His Majesty the King. "I think I shall go to the moon."

"My dear," said the Queen, "the moon is much too high."

3

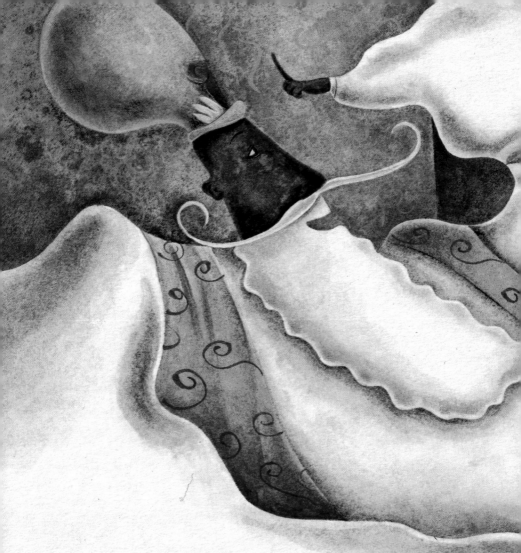

"Don't be silly," said the King. "I'm His Majesty
the King. Nothing is too high for me."

"You will need a very long ladder," said the Queen.

"Don't be silly," said the King. "I'm His Majesty
the King. I'm not climbing to the moon on
a ladder!"

4

"Silly me," said the Queen. "What you need is a tower."

"Just the thing," said the King. "Bring me boxes!"

All the people came with boxes. Then they went
and got some more.

"More boxes!" cried the King. "I'm His
Majesty the King and tonight I shall climb up
to the moon."

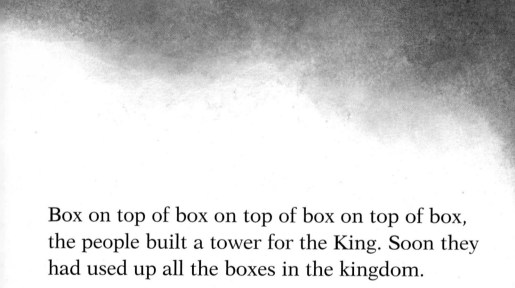

Box on top of box on top of box on top of box, the people built a tower for the King. Soon they had used up all the boxes in the kingdom.

The King looked up at the tower. "Are you coming, too?" he asked the Queen.

"No thanks," she said. "I'll stay here."

So the King had to climb the tower all by himself.

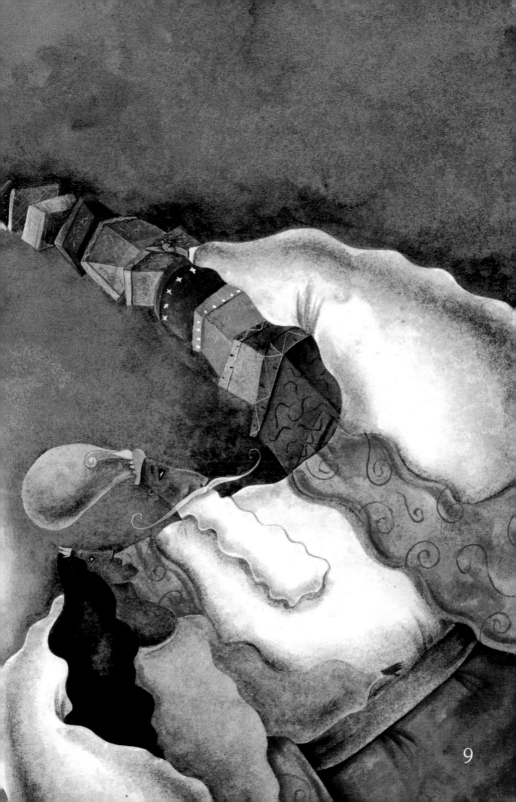

When he got to the top, he wobbled a lot, and so did the crown on his head.

"I did it!" he said. Then he stood up on one leg and tried to reach the moon.

"I need one more box!" he cried. "This tower isn't high enough to get me to the moon."

10

But there weren't any more boxes.

"Take the box from the bottom and put it up on top," cried the King.

"Don't be silly!" said the Queen.

"Oh, no!" the people cried.

12

The people pulled the box out
and the tower and the King came
tumbling down. So did his crown.

"Silly me," said the King,
as he rubbed his head.

14

15

"My dear," said the Queen, "it's a beautiful night.
Let's go to sleep."

16